Attercliffe

another wander up the 'cliffe

Text copyright 2003 © Michael Liversidge

Photographic copyright © Michael Liversidge, Jack Wrigley, David Richardson Collection

along with various others - credited at picture source

ISBN 0 9544045 5 6

Printed in 2003 by Pickard Communication

Published & Printed by Pickard Communication

10-11 Riverside Park

Sheaf Gardens

Sheffield S2 4BB

Telephone 0114 275 7222 or 275 7444

email info@picomm.co.uk

www.picomm.co.uk

contents

attercliffe common ends at weedon street
and starts at kirkbridge road

attercliffe road ends at kirkbridge road
and starts at twelve o'clock court

Introduction

After "A Wander up the 'Cliffe" was printed and published, I sat back in the knowledge that my "literary days" were numbered. So it may come as somewhat of a surprise to find my second book on Attercliffe for sale in the shops, it is to me!

"A Wander up the 'Cliffe" was fairly well received, obviously mainly by ex Attercliffe residents and from its Sheffield Star Diary Page launch on 2/12/2001 I have been on the receiving end of many letters, emails and telephone calls. Mostly, thank goodness, saying how good it was to recall all the old places and for some people the old faces which were depicted in the book.

Along with this rather pleasing response came a rather unforeseen bonus - anecdotes, family stories (histories) and pictures were offered, some from as far afield as Australia and America. From much nearer home came Reverend Frank Hone who contacted me about a picture, in a wander up the cliffe, on page 42, of him leading the church procession down Attercliffe Road towards Attercliffe Common. After a couple of letters and phone calls Reverend and Mrs Hone invited me to their home in rural Lincolnshire. Besides their very kind hospitality, they showed me pictures of their time at Attercliffe Church in the mid to late 50s and pictures of their stay at Brightside Church. A couple of Rev Hones pictures really capture what Attercliffe was like in the 1950s.

So it is armed with these generous gifts and with more photographic help from a couple of good friends Jack Wrigley and David Richardson that I set out on **"Another wander up the Cliffe"**.

New pictures, new stories, less personal details, thank goodness - I hear you say, and a different year from the local directory, 1963 this time.

A hairdresser (barber) - lady doctor - vicar - schoolteacher who is also a nationally known sports coach - a print company director - policeman - and a couple of businessmen who owned Attercliffe premises - all remember their times down Attercliffe.

Another wander up the Cliffe will not be laid out quite as rigidly in the geographical context the previous book was, going from Weedon Street up towards the 12 O'clock pub finish, but I will try to keep some semblance of Common to Road format.

I hope you enjoy

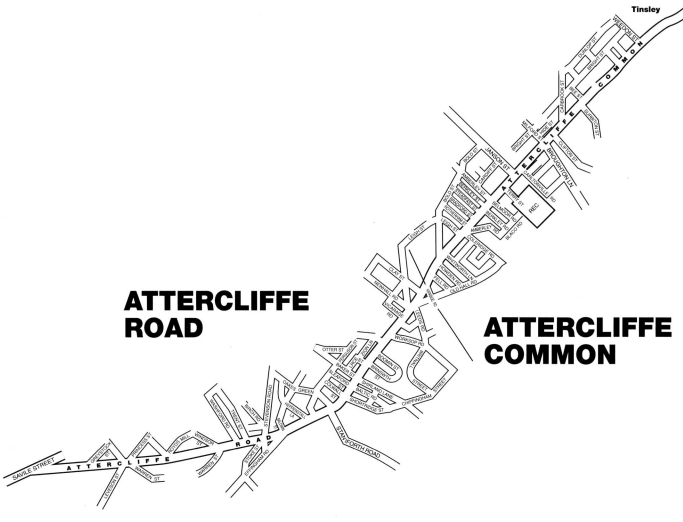

ATTERCLIFFE ROAD

ATTERCLIFFE COMMON

Tinsley Park Colliery

Though not in Attercliffe the colliery did employ a large amount of men from Attercliffe and as such I think warrants a mention. The Tinsley Park Colliery closed six years before I was born in 1943, when during the war years it experienced difficulties, not only in the fact men were off on military service but also the very stringent air raid black outs. Coke could only be drawn from the ovens in daylight, this was especially crucial in the Sheffield area were the nearby steel firm was a major Luftwaffe target. The Ministry of Fuel and Power, in its wisdom, closed the pit "in the national interest". Tinsley Park itself was difficult to get to, as it was a half mile walk from Weedon Street up Billy Cooks Lane and over the canal and railway and through allotments. It had no public transport service as well as the ultimate problem no public house. Another way in or out was through Tinsley Park Road and Cuddy Meadows on to Greenland Road. The Colliery did provide something I remember well, Little Wembley, a slight misnomer, but still the best pitch in the area.

My early secondary education at Coleridge Road School had Friday morning football sessions, generally with teachers who did not want to make the walk to LIttle Wembley, which was a good half-a-mile from the school. We went in all weathers and took 2 classes, around 58-60 kids in double file. Whilst the skillful future Peles showed their class on the two pitches the rest were left to kick about on their own, generally with the soft football.

Mr Knowles one of the teachers who made the trip, somewhat begrudgingly, called the less talented players the "dirty dozen" or the "tin can dribblers". Politically incorrect these days, but Fred Knowles never bothered with any of that rubbish. If a kid wasn't good at something, be it sport, maths, English, history, geography, or any other subject our Fred told him so.

Harry the Barber

In *A wander up the Cliffe* I mentioned with some affection Harry the Barber whose shop was at 333 Attercliffe Common next door to the Carbrook Conservative Club. A few months after publication I received a very nice letter from Australia from the hairdresser who sold Harry his shop in 1955. To complicate matters his name was Harry (Burnham). So before Harry the Barbers it was Harry the Barbers! No wonder I was confused as a kid.

Sheffield's New President

Mr. H. Burnham

Mr. HARRY BURNHAM, newly-elected President of Sheffield Branch NHF, came out of the Services with the intention of starting in business on his own account. He did so and, at the same time, joined the Federation. His rise to the highest office in the branch has been a rapid one, which has proved his fitness for the task and his popularity. One of his main objects will be to increase membership, as was that of his predecessor. Mr. W. D. HEWITT, who was very successful.

Mr. Burnham took over the business in a densely populated area, from Mr JOHN HENRY MILLS who had more than half a century in the Trade.

above:
Harry and his wife along with family, celebrating their 55th wedding anniversary, down under.

right:
A newspaper clipping of Harry Burnham

below:
The interior of Harry the Barbers
333 Attercliffe Common
Photographs: Harry Burnham

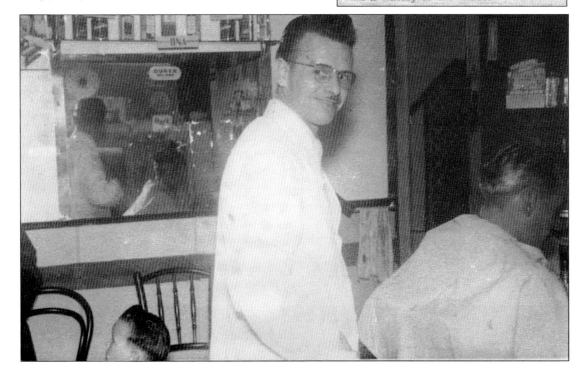

Dr Ivy Oates

Ivy Oates was born during the First World War, 1916, and worked as an army doctor in World War II. She arrived in Sheffield in 1951 and in the years that followed she ran medical practices in Carbrook, Wadsley Bridge, Foxhill and Shiregreen.

A mother of four children, Dr Oates started her Attercliffe medical duties in the early fifties in partnership with Dr Labib Botros, but very quickly moved on to work in her own practice at the side of the Carbrook Hall. She worked without the aid of the telephone - I am led to believe that any emergencies would come through to the Carbrook Hall Garage and be passed on immediately. One story she related to me was that of an old woman who was blind and did not want to leave the Attercliffe area when the slum clearance got under way. As is the norm in these cases the council won the day and the lady was moved on to the estates, Parson Cross, I believe. Upon entering her new abode she stated what a lovely colour yellow the curtains were. To everyone's amazement it was discovered she was not totally blind as was thought for many years, it was just that it was so dark and overcast in that area of Carbrook she could not distinguish colours or items in general.

The Open University's longest serving student, Dr Oates had gained degrees in the fields

of Science and Art, Health, Social Welfare and History. This incredible woman is still very active as an after dinner speaker.

left:
Dr Oates with her children

below:
A recent picture of Ivy Oates in her Chapeltown home
Photographs: Ivy Oates

Carbrook Elementary School

Miss Middleton was head at this school in all my time there and I am led to believe that she was the first woman headteacher at any Junior School in Sheffield. She took charge in 1954 and was still headteacher well into the 1960s.

Veda Gwendoline Middleton to give her her full name was born on Infirmary Road, at the George the IV where it was reputed her father was the only teetotal landlord in Sheffield.

Miss Middleton's brother, Desmond Peter, was one of the founder members of the 1st Special Air Services (SAS) and served under Colonel Paddy Mayne from June 1942 until November 1945. He took part in the Western Desert, Italy and North West Europe Campaigns.

It was detailed in my last book that the old infant part of the school was turned into the Players Cafe Bar - sadly in the short time since then it has hit hard times and closed. At the present time (September 2003) it is being used as a canteen for a company whose premises are situated nearby.

left:
Veda Middleton

below :
Players Cafe interior which was previously the Carbrook Infants School

The Attercliffe Windmill (pub and landmark)

I cannot say I know the history of the Attercliffe windmill. In fact until I saw a painting by Edward J Vickers, in the last year or so, on exhibition at Renishaw Hall I did not even know of its existence.

The windmill was surrounded by twelve acres of land which extended along the riverside near to the present day Amberley Street. I have found separate articles, one states that the mill was built in 1811, the second suggests it was built much earlier. The tall chimney which was erected near this site when steam power came into being was built in 1832. It seems to have been owned by the Hill family from 1811 until 1855. Firstly, James and then George Hill, both Corn Millers, owned the Don Bank House which was situated next to the Windmill.

A little piece I found on the internet may give some idea of Attercliffe two centuries ago.

A Walk Through Attercliffe in 1806

The writer of this piece describing a walk in Attercliffe in 1806 is unknown, he simply signed himself as one of Attercliffe's oldest inhabitants.

In 1806 the immediate surroundings were those of rural beauty and its scenery of wood and dale, of hill and water, was of the most pleasing character. The clear flowing Don was well stocked with a variety of fish and on both sides of the river were large and magnificent trees. The village was studded with plantations and orchards, fruit trees overhanging the footpath on many parts of the main road.

Walking through Attercliffe at that time and starting at Washford Bridge at the Sheffield end of the village, one would first see at the back of a row of houses newly erected on the cliff running sheer above the Don, the remains of a very old house occupied by Jonathon Oakes, a scissor manufacturer. Nearby was Blast Lane, so called from the blast furnaces that stood there. There also was the home of Mark Oakes, a crucible maker. Up Bacon Lane and over the canal bridge, was a large brick house built by William Blagden, builder of boats and barges at the Sheffield Canal Basin. Nearby were the extensive grounds and stables occupied by William Wright, of the King's Head Hotel, Change Alley, for the breeding and training of race horses. Mr Wright also trained piebald horses for circus performances! A large field opposite Mr Blagden's house was used for the annual Attercliffe Races.

A little higher up the lane was the entrance to the ornamental grounds, flower and kitchen gardens, in the centre of which stood the fine mansion, Woodburn House. This was the residence of Henry Sorby of the firm J. Sorby and Sons in Spital Hill. Retracing our steps to the main road, we would have seen on our left the old corn mill and mansion of John Shirley, miller, corn merchant and maltster. Delightful gardens stretched up the road. Nearby was the old Green Dragon, occupied by George Drabble, a notable character. Over the way was the Hope and Anchor, kept by Benjamin Blythe, and a little further on, the Robin Hood, occupied by Isaac Bailey, a file grinder. Almost immediately opposite was Carlton House, a fine building and residence of Samuel Jackson, of the firm Spear and Jackson. The grounds of this house were very extensive, occupying a large space fronting the main road and also considerable distance down Oakes Green. The grounds contained plantations of fine trees, flower gardens and a pleasant fish pond.

Bull and bear baiting were carried on until about this period. The bouts were staged at the annual village feast, held in a field at the bottom of Oakes Green, near the river. These cruel sports were finally ended when a bear killed it's owner, a man named Runcorn.

A little beyond Oakes Green, on the same side, was a fine brick house occupied by the Misses Green as 'Ladies Seminary'. On the left was the old public house, the Horse and Jockey, kept for many years by George Twigg. A little further on was the house of Dr Richardson, who was a great favourite with his patients. Crossing over Back Lane (now Shirland Lane) we would have seen the public house known as The Queen's Head, whose landlord was Jake Smith. Back again, to the left, was the residence of Charles Hancock. This house had a large front garden, orchard and wood, in which there was a big rookery. On the right was the old established shop of Benjamin Johnson, one of the three boot and shoe makers in Attercliffe. Further on, the Masons' Arms was occupied by George Hague, an old native of the village, whilst nearby were the wheelrights shops of Billy and Bobby Goodwin. A little further on were the stack yard and farm buildings of David Deakin, who was a well liked farmer.

Crossing over the road again, we would have seen the Wesleyan Chapel, this, with Zion, were the only Nonconformist places of worship in the village. Near the Wesleyan Chapel was Thomas Fawley's butchers shop, whilst next door was the Coach and Horses, one of the oldest public houses, occupied by Tommy Corker, a joiner by trade. At the corner of Worksop Road was a house and shop owned by Philip Whitham, who was a grocer and tallow chandler. Next was the Travellers Inn, a most respectable public house, occupied by William Banks, then next door the workshops of John Hawksworth, pen and pocket knife manufacturer.

Retracing our steps back to Church Street (now Attercliffe Road) we would have seen the residence Benjamin Hancock, fender manufacturer. Nearby, standing in its own grounds, was the fine stone mansion erected by Mr. F. Huntsman, steel manufacturer. He was the great grandson of Benjamin Huntsman, the inventor of crucible steel.

A little way above was the Old Blue Bell public house, occupied by Molly Whiteley and her son Billy. Over the road we would have seen the Old Bowling Green public house whose landlord was Sally Wheatman. This was a favourite resort by many of the respectable inhabitants of the village, for there could be enjoyed a very good game of bowls. Nearby was the Plough Inn kept by Billy Grey, who was also employed by the firm of Huntsman as a steel smelter.

We would then come to the mansion and grounds of the Milner family. Gamabiel Milner was a fine old English gentleman who commanded the respect and esteem of all who knew him. Again on the main road, we would have seen the Golden Ball public house, occupied by George Watson, who was also a butcher. Next was the brick house and workshop of William Parker, a spade and shovel maker.

A little further on we reach New Hall Estate, which was the seat of Mr. Swallow, iron founder. Here were plantations extending from the Vicarage to the commencement of Attercliffe Common. A stone lodge stood on either side of the Estate entrance, with large gates between. These opened on to a splendid coach drive down to the Hall, with an avenue of fine trees on either side. (This drive is now Newhall Road). Standing on Swallow Bridge over the Don, the view is perfect! The Hall was surrounded by trees and large pleasure grounds. Orchards were stacked with rich fruit trees, there were massive flower gardens and a large shrubbery. Past the house was a wood and rockery and then extensive meadows full of cattle. The clean and silvery Don, it's banks occupied by lofty trees overhanging the water, was a most picturesque site.

Retracing our steps to the main road again, we would have found on the left hand at Hill Top the residence and workshops of William Walkland, a wheelwright, whose family was of long standing in Attercliffe. Not far from Walkland's was an old house situated at the top of a garden, where lived Samuel Foster, a noted chisel maker. A couple of hundred yards further on we would have come to the Old Chapel, built in 1629, and its extensive burial ground.

Nearby was the old windmill, with its house and a good garden. George Hill was the miller and corn factor. Across the road was Pot House Lane and there we would have seen the dwelling and a pottery worked by William Fearnley. Next we should come to Broughton Lane, named after Spence Broughton, the robber whose body was hung here in chains on a gibbet for thirty six years!

We finish our walk at Carbrook Hall, occupied by George Bradford, the largest farmer in the district.

A very interesting piece of Attercliffe History. Note all the public houses that were still in situ all the way through until the 1970. Green Dragon, Hope and Anchor (Sportman), Coach and Horses (Swan Hotel), Travellers Inn, a most respectable public house, Golden Ball and the Carbrook Hall.

The Attercliffe Windmill (pub and landmark)

There used to be a public house called the Windmill Inn at 30/32 Amberley Street. This was possibly so called because of the close proximity to the Windmill on Bold Street. The public house itself was sited on the corner of Amberley Street and Cardiff Street (formerly Queen Street) and over the years it was looked after by Mr John Bailey, grocer and beerkeeper in 1871; Mr George Whitworth also grocer and beerkeeper in 1881 and then it states Mr George Whitworth was the publican in 1891; Mr George Solomon Brookes beerhouse keeper; Mr George Redford just registered as a beerhouse in 1905-1920; and possibly the last tenant whilst a public house was Mrs Mary Jane Radford 1930-1931.

Many years later, in the 1950s, when I called at my friends Lee and Grant Froggatt, who lived on Amberley Street, the old pub was no more and it was Mrs Bamford who kept it as a grocers and sweet shop.

Amberley Hotel at the joining of Amberley St with Attercliffe Common

The Attercliffe Windmill situated on Bold Street

13

Betty Cordona (nee Cutts)

Betty Cutts lived next door to my family at 34 Belmoor Road. She became a teacher at Hatfield House Lane School at Shiregreen and was a founder of the most successful side in British Sport - The Sheffield Hatters - Women's Basketball.

This side has won all the major trophies on offer and for a few years were basically unbeatable. Betty played for many years for the Hatters and then became their coach which she still is to this day. She was also the National Coach for some time.

Betty's mother and father owned the grocers shop (pictured below) on Attercliffe Common as well as a Turf Accountants. My father, Joe Liversidge, uncle Ron Otley and a close friend of mine Allan Dent used to spend all day Saturday trying to take Frank's money. They never learnt: Raceform Notebook, Handicap News, tipsters they tried the lot and it never gained them a penny. I am sure Frank Cutts used to rub his hands in glee when he saw those three walk in his shop.

left:
Betty playing for the Hatters

right:
Cutts Turf accountants just beyond the Amberley and Filesmiths pubs.

below :
Maud Cutts stood outside her shop - Flathers chippy to her left

above:
The Sheffield Hatters in their infancy

below:
Betty Cordona with her daughters after receiving her OBE at Buckingham Palace

Iris Taylor - Scofton Place

At a Coleridge Road School reunion at the Carbrook Hall public house, a childhood friend, Iris Taylor (now Iris Greenhedge) chatted to me about the old times, and old friends down Attercliffe. Iris also stated she had some photographs of when she was a child living in Scofton Place (a cul-de-sac off Belmoor Road). She has kindly let me reproduce them over the next few pages.

left:
Iris in Charlie Bartons arms feeding the Co-op Horse with bread on Scofton Place.

below:
A spillage on Scofton Place.
The Co-op milk horse looks on.

above:
Iris with young friend stood in front of the drinking fountain in Carbrook Recreation Ground. The park keeper's house looming large in the background. The grassless football area is on the extreme left.

below:
Joyce Hague with son Martin (in car) stood with Lois Hague (no relation) in Scofton Place back yard. The houses in the background were the backs of the homes on Terry Street

The Blitz

Sheffield had two nights of hell on the 12th-13th and 15-16th December 1940. Before those two fateful nights most people, those who weren't on military service, had read about the war in Europe and possibly reflected on how it was always a city in France or Belgium that would be bombed. As English cities became bombing targets, the unsettling thought occurred that with all our industry and armaments production, Sheffield would become a major target. Even after the Battle of Britain, which cheered many people, it was thought the Germans would continue with their deadly night-time visits. Carbrook and Tinsley had a September raid in which three people died. But December 1940 saw the real force of the Luftwaffe over our city. One would have thought that Attercliffe, with its swathe of steel firms would have been the main target of the German air force on those nights, but in all honesty it got off with less bombs dropped on it than the city centre, Pitsmoor and the Brincliffe and Highfield areas of Sheffield. Attercliffe still had over 40 bombs to deal with and these caused death and destruction on possibly a bigger scale because of the close proximity of the housing. In a residential area were the housing was detached or semi detached a bomb would possibly destroy one or two properties. If a bomb hit in the Attercliffe area it could take out half a street. My father's house on Mountain Street was completely destroyed along with a few neighbouring properties. He and his family were rehoused in Clinton Place, off Ecclesall Road.

In all, 602 people died in Sheffield on those two horrendous nights.

*Birch Road
after the blitz*

Marples

Whilst the Marples public house is not situated in the Attercliffe area, when it was devastated by German bombs on the night of 12th December 1940 four local women were to lose their lives there.

Ethel Beardshaw, aged 27, of Fowler Terrace, Ada Buxton, aged 35, and Elsie Siddall, aged 45, both of 144 Sutherland Road and Mabel Dean, aged 30, of 14 Kimberley Street all met their end along with 66 more victims. A larger proportion of women than men died in the Marples bombing.

The London Mart (the correct name for the public house) received a direct hit from a Luftwaffe bomber. Of the 77 staff and customers who were there on that fateful night only

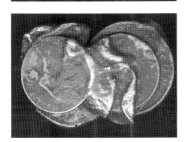

seven were pulled out alive by local miners especially called in to help with the rescue.

A good friend, Pete Barker, has some coins which were found at the scene of the bombing and were welded together with the intense heat.

above:
Coins found in the Marples aftermath

left:
An illustration of The London Mart public house

right:
The interior - The Snack Bar

Football in Attercliffe

A club that started life in 1870 as **Christ Church** (it became **Attercliffe FC** in 1873/74 season) was considered one of the area's larger clubs in the latter part of the 19th century. The team actually only reached one major local final, losing the 1879 Challenge cup to Wednesday. it did win several of the minor trophies that were up for grabs in the period leading up to the turn of the century. Attercliffe FC's first ground was on Shirland Lane before moving to the Forge Ground on Brightside Lane. This was an athletics ground with the pitch encircled by the running track. In season 1881/82, Attercliffe provided four players for the Sheffield FA team. They were Robinson, Marsden, Barber and Beardshaw.

Sheffield FC, the oldest organised football club in the world, played down at the new Don Valley stadium for a while in the late 1990s.

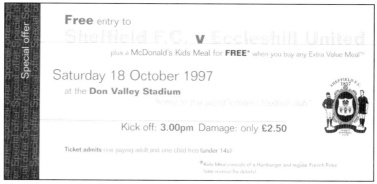

Free entry to

Sheffield F.C. v Eccleshill United

plus a McDonald's Kids Meal for **FREE*** when you buy any Extra Value Meal™

Saturday 18 October 1997
at the **Don Valley Stadium**
"home to the world's oldest football club"

Kick off: **3.00pm** Damage: only **£2.50**

Ticket admits one paying adult and one child free (under 14s)

*Kids Meal consists of a Hamburger and regular French Fries
(see reverse for details)

Sheffield FC a ticket to their match against Eccleshill United in 1997

Not exactly on the actual playing side, but a recent addition to the Board of Directors at Sheffield Wednesday was also an Attercliffe lad, Kenneth Cooke, who lived on Scofton Place and used to kick about on the old Carbrook rec with Paul Smedley and myself.

Also one of the many Attercliffe pub teams I played for in the sixties, the Bird in Hand, were winners of a trophy in 1913 called the Sheffield Licensed Victuallers Challenge Cup (pictured right). Now I do not know who sold this item (and who would be able to sell something that was obviously set up to be played for annually) but in May 2002 it was put up for sale at Sotherbys. It is detailed thus. A massive Edwardian silver plated trophy cup and cover and a silver plated trophy shield - this item was sold to a private buyer for nearly £8000. I approached Sotherbys to view the said item and was told it had already been sold to a private buyer and was not available to view. The Sheffield and Hallamshire Football Association and various leagues in Sheffield surely should have looked into buying this prestigious item for posterity or at least the Sheffield Museums should have taken an interest in keeping this lovely trophy to be viewed by the people of Sheffield. I have written to the Sheffield Star to see if they can see who sold or who bought said item but as yet have received no reply.

The Trophy

Football

Almost all the pubs, clubs and steel companies on Attercliffe had their own football team, such as Hadfields and English Steel. Both of these firms had their ground on Bawtry Road. Brown Bayleys, had pitches on Oliver's Mount, Handsworth. All used to have three or four teams in the Hatchard League, Works League, Beatty League, Works Minor etc. If you started at one of the steel companies you were invariably asked on your first day not about the skills you could put into the job, but "weers tha play then lad, goalie, at back, up front".

You found the chap who ran the football teams knew when new lads were starting and made sure he approached them as soon as was possible.

I did not work for them, but I played for many years for Hadfields and then Bayfields in the Sheffield Hatchard League.

Top:
Hadfield FC who played in the Sheffield Hatchard League
This picture was taken in the mid 1970s.
Standing: Stuart Wright, Bob Whistowski, Dave Wilde, Mick Liversidge, Terry Lees, Ralph Bond, Alan Mills.
Front: Tony Hodgkinson, Paul Dore, Martin Hannah, Mark Liversidge Mascot, Roy Hannaby and Derrick Hindley

Middle:
Brown Bayleys football team in the 1927 season

Below:
Still playing, well turning out, aged 54, for William Hills in first Division of Regional Alliance Sunday League. M Liversidge back row 3rd from left

Other Sports in Attercliffe

The World Student Games of 1991 split the good people of Sheffield. Was it a good idea to create sporting stadia with the obvious follow on of amenities and facilities, or a complete waste of rate payers money, of which there was plenty spent.

Not an argument you want to get caught up in, as the debate can still become quite heated. I will let you, the reader, decide.

Some other sports have tried to become the people's favourite. We have Ice Hockey: The Sheffield Steelers; American Football: the Spartans; Rugby League: Sheffield Eagles; Women's Basketball: The Hatters; Mens Basketball: The Sheffield Sharks have all tried their luck in the new Arenas and Stadium that were built for the 1991 games.

above and below: The World Student Games came to Attercliffe, Sheffield in 1991.

left:
Spartans, American Football.
Ticket for Don Valley Stadium

below left:
The programme for Sheffield Steelers in their first competitive match at the Arena in 1991

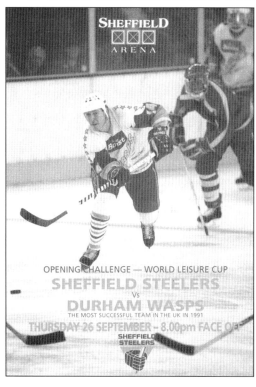

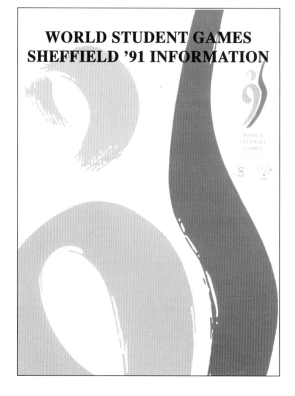

Paul Smedley

Paul Smedley and I, along with the rest of our gang, Dickie Martin, Linda Cutts, Susan Pearson, and Paul's younger sister Janet were a group of youngsters who all lived in close proximity and were inseparable in our formative years.

Paul Smedley left Coleridge Road School and had a brief spell in printing and tailoring before joining Sheffield City Police at the age of 16 as a Cadet. He served his time as a Cadet at West Bar, Woodseats, Attercliffe (which was handy) and Rotherham traffic division, eventually becoming P.C.1119 and leaving for the thirteen-week training course at Panel Ash, near Harrogate.

It was during this time that he acquired his first car a Ford Classic Capri. This car carried Pete Glossop, Kenny Taylor and Paul as a learner driver to and from Panel at the weekends.

On one memorable occasion his sister, Janet, decided that she wanted to learn to drive and under the instruction of another young policeman, Russ Jackson, she crashed it and left it parked outside their house, 18 Belmoor Road, for Paul to find.

Paul's family eventually left Attercliffe, as everybody did in 1970, and with his mum, dad and sister Janet moved to Hollybank Crescent at Intake. Some months after he had left, and at the end of a busy and tiring night shift, Paul found myself turning the Capri into Belmoor Road having forgotten he had moved.

Whilst Paul was stationed at West Bar one Saturday morning in January 1972, he was sent to Pitsmoor Post office where there had been a report of a robbery by two men one of which was believed to have a knife. He went around the back of Pitsmoor Road and came

across a man answering the description of one of the offenders. He pointed the "knife" directly at PC Smedley and it went bang. It was a gun. He missed and made an attempt to get away running towards Shirecliffe Lane. Paul eventually caught up with him after what seemed a marathon, Paul's words not mine (running had never been his strong point) and he was overpowered and arrested with the assistance of other officers. For this act of Bravery, Paul Smedley received a Judge's Commendation, the only Sheffield and Rotherham Constabulary Award for Bravery ever awarded and the story made the front page of the Star.

PC Paul Smedley

He was eventually posted to Attercliffe in 1976 and had three great years at Whitworth Lane where he continued the art of "Bobbying" something that unfortunately has been lost in today's modern Police Service. Whilst on the beat one day he was told a story by an old lady in Brightside who knew his mum, Betsy Smedley. She told him a story his mother had never told them. During the war, as a young girl living with her parents, Betsy got a job as a silver service waitress at the Marples in Fitzalan Square. That was fine by her father. However Betsy realised she could earn more money at William Cooks Foundry (locally known as Billy Cooks). She would leave home dressed in her white blouse, black skirt, carrying her pini, white gloves and bag. As soon as she got on to the bus she would put on her overalls and go to work at Bill Cooks. All went well until, as history shows, the Marples took a direct hit during the Blitz on Sheffield, with a tragic loss of life. Betsy, ignorant of what had happened, came home after her shift dressed in her white blouse and black skirt to face grieving parents who gave her a clip round the ear for being alive! She continued to work at Billy Cooks and it was on one of the works' outings to Skegness that she met Paul's dad, a flight sergeant and gunner in the R.A.F.

In 1979, Paul was posted to Rotherham traffic Division at Masborough Street. In this period he dealt with eleven fatal road accidents, in a fourteen-month period, on both motorways and A roads. Paul relates "In those days we just got on with it and relied on the support of our mates". The worst part was informing the relatives. Nowadays, he states "such trauma requires counselling and long periods of sick leave, followed by a claim for damages".

In November 1984 Paul was assaulted whilst walking a beat in Doncaster Town Centre. This resulted in him being pensioned from the Force in 1985. He still suffers with Tinnitus and hearing impairment to this day.

left:
George Smedley - Paul's father, showing him how to ride his trike

top: Paul and myself sitting on the wall - note the compulsary cricket wicket chalked on the bricks

After some 10 months of convalescing and looking for work, in 1986 he eventually found a job with the Cooperative Wholesale Society as a Security Supervisor at the Claywheels Lane Distribution Depot. Between then and 1999 he worked for the C.W.S in Merseyside, South Wales and Manchester. In 1995 he became the Deputy Head of Security and had

Above: Kevin Sykes and Janet Smedley do the Co-op milk run

responsibility for the Commercial Division. Soon after he started that job he was with his dad, George, when he collapsed and died in Paul's arms. Betsy, Paul's mum never really recovered and she, sadly, died two years after.

His previous experience as a policeman was a good grounding for what was to become his second career and he probably dealt with as much crime, and certainly more serious fraud, whilst with the C.W.S.

After living for about eleven years in and around Manchester (not an experience, he says, he wishes to repeat), he now lives with his wife Christine in Barnsley, with his two adopted daughters, Kirsty and Heidi, who are both grown up. Paul is now the proud grandfather of Katherine who has just had her first birthday.

For the time being Paul still works in Manchester as a Crime Reduction Advisor to the Commercial Sector on Trafford Park, but who knows he may come full circle and finish up doing the same thing back down the 'Cliffe.

Olivers Butchers

Mr Bernard Oliver telephoned one day and asked if I would send him an Attercliffe book. This I duly did, and in the packaging I asked if he lived down the Cliffe and various other questions. It turned out that Bernard is one of the Olivers butchers who seemed to have a shop every 50 yards all the way up the Common. I think they actually had seven butchers in the area. He kindly sent me the picture of his extended family outside their various butchers. The tall gentleman on the left, standing outside the shop carrying the motto the People Butchers, is Bernard's father. This shop was actually in

Grimesthorpe Road. I think the other old photograph is on Attercliffe Road before the numbers were changed. I am led to believe initially the business started as Oliver Bros of which there were four in total. Then there was Edward Oliver and sons, actually nine sons and five daughters. All of the sons became butchers and four of the sisters helped in the shops and on the vans. Bernard thinks this family lived on Freeston Place off Leigh Street. All the sons are now deceased, except for Richard, the youngest, plus three of the sisters, one of whom lives in Canada and is now 99 years old. The other two sisters live locally in or around the Rotherham area. Some family!

above:
Bernard Oliver's father outside his shop in Grimesthorpe Road

below:
Eight of the nine Oliver brothers only Richard (the youngest) is missing
Photographs: B Oliver

*One of
Olivers shops*

*below:
Olivers shop
facing Banners
on Attercliffe
Road*

Photographs:
Bernard Oliver

Arthur Wood and Roger Midlane

When I started work at Fred Mellings Printers on Zion Lane, Arthur and Roger, both Attercliffe lads, were already well established and both proficient journeymen compositors. A Compositor is (or was) the person who puts type together letter by letter as can be seen in the photograph below of someone composing type into a printers pye-stick.

For about eight years from being 16 years of age until I moved on to another printing firm I was their apprentice for five years and a journeyman, myslef, for three years. Roger and I played for various local football teams, including Grimesthorpe Old Boys, The Pheasant, Meadowhall Road, the Roman Ridge, Wincobank and Woodhouse West End. Roger, who originally came from Liverpool Street was a very talented footballer, a right winger with pace and ability. They don't make 'em like that any more - ask Sheffield Wednesday, they haven't had a good one for years.

Typecase and compositor

Arthur used to live in Attercliffe up the top end, as we used to say, near Heppenstall Lane and Carlton House. He once told me one of the shop around that area, Taylor's Old junk shop, had a full Samurai warrior's suit of armour and sword. The chap used to put it outside his shop every morning and take it in at night. I bet it was a lovely colour stood out in the Attercliffe elements. A suit like that would be worth a small fortune now. Also he told of an old scrap man who used to take his donkey down a few steps and into his house which had straw festooned on the floor. They nicknamed this man Donkey Jack, well you would wouldn't you.

One of Arthur's passion was shooting, and he competed at Bisley for many years.

left: Mellings Printers on Zion Lane

right: Arthur Wood

Reverend Frank Hone

Reverend Hone served churches at Attercliffe, Brightside and the Manor areas of Sheffield during the 50s and early 60s.

Along with his wife and two children, a son and daughter, Frank lived in all these areas (the longest period at Attercliffe) before moving away from Sheffield to carry on his work with the church

Frank Hone had possibly more contact with the Attercliffe public than most, he took services, often sorted the churchgoers personal problems, arranged meeting of all kinds, was even asked to be in charge of the Pakistani community group, helped with the less fortunates, was in charge of the local church football team and he arranged trips, outings etc.

Reverend Frank Hone with his new (second hand) Austin which cost around £160
Photo Frank Hone

Pakistan Day - six Pakistani gentlemen outside the Attercliffe Church gardens.
Photo Frank Hone

Parade passing Attercliffe Shops - Stop the H Bomb float - Reverend Hone's attempt to show the folly of man's infatuation with weapons of mass destruction, for which he was later chastised.
Photo Frank Hone

Reverend Hone and friends on an Alton Towers outing - I think this was his Brightside congregation.
Photo Frank Hone

Smokey Attercliffe, photo taken from Brightside churchyard early 50s
Photo Frank Hone

Looking down towards Weedon Street? Beer being delivered on the left and a future brickie on the right
Photo Frank Hone

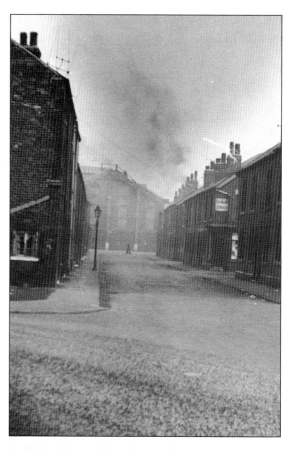

A foggy day down Attercliffe.
possibly a tram or bus stop or both!
Photo Frank Hone

Is this looking up Mons Street, Southern Street?
Photo Frank Hone

Slightly off the beaten track of Attercliffe but this picture of a Whit Monday procession getting ready for the off is of the now demolished Adsetts Street off Upwell Street. You can just make out the Prince of Wales pub on the left of picture

St Thomas Football Team, Sheffield Bible Class League in the early 50s
F Hone, Colin Christian, Smail, and Jackson are the only names that can be recalled.
Photo Frank Hone

At the rear of the graveyard

The war memorial stone still in the Attercliffe church grounds

Stuart Green

Stuart Green, someone who I have only recently met through another local book publication **Forty Years On,** a story about the technical college on Leopold Street, very kindly supplied me with some marvellous pictures and some nice stories about the steel firm that stretched all along the part of Attercliffe where I lived.

above: Worksop Road from the Aqueduct bridge

below: The Cocked Hat, Leeds Road and Brown Bayleys Offices

Brown Bayley

Brown Bayley's was one of the biggest employers on Attercliffe, at one time it employed 3,000 workers on its vast 36 acres worksite. Its place in British history is assured with vital components being made here for Allcock and Browns atlantic flight, for the airship R101 as well as Concord. During the Second World War, the company supplied more than 9,000 big gun barrels and more than one million rifles.

Work began on the site in September 1871, as soon as the grain harvest from the fields was in. Attercliffe was very rural then. The factory was built near the station on the South Yorkshire Railway, between Pothouse Lane (now Coleridge Road) and the Darnall Turnpike (now Worksop road). The railway and the canal formed the back boundaries.

The immediate workforce was to be 1,500. The buildings were a machine and buffer shop, shops for hammers, wheels, forges; a smithy with 50 fitters, and Bessemer steel house with four converter vessels capable of turning out 1,200 tons a week The rail mill was to be one of the biggest in the world.

There is some doubt about the firm's proper name. It was known as George Brown's but it was described in Sheffield Independent as Brown, Bayley and Dixon. Two years later it became a limited company set up by Joseph Dixon, John Clowes Bayley and George Brown. A lab was added and it was here that John Arnold, who later became professor of Metallurgy at the university, was sent as a lad to learn the business.

Harry Brearley, the discoverer of stainless steel, joined the firm as technical director in 1915.

December 15 1940, saw a land mine land on No 1 mill. Repairs took nearly a year and in the meantime the company's ingots had to be sent all over the country for rolling.

Like the rest of the steel industry Brown Bayleys struggled through the seventies and finally in the mid 1980s it ceased to trade.

In 1985, its 100 ton electric arc furnace, rated the most modern in Europe. was being shipped off to Turkey. For some strange reason the Turkish flag fluttered form the roof of the derelict works.

The Friends and Adults school.

Brown Bayley was taken over by Hadfields - ultimately Lonrho - but still within a few years the whole place had closed.

Numbers of schemes were put forward for the site. Gleesons wanted to build houses; the city council thought the area suitable for parkland. It was not until serious planning began for the World Student Games in 1991 that the idea of the athletics stadium arose.

So after 120 years of looming large over Attercliffe, the structures of Brown Bayleys ceased to exist and on part of its many acres was built the Don Valley Stadium.

Some of the names destined to become world famous as steel makers actually began in Sheffield's lighter trades. For instance, Charles Cammell started as a file maker, John Brown was a cutlery factor, and Firth's early products included files, saws and edge tools.

top:
A cobbled Coleridge Road. Brown Bayley's entrance on the left of picture. Old Hall Road on the right.

left:
Old Hall Road near its junction with Attercliffe Road and Leeds Road.

above: Centinal at work and below one of the vehicle being kept in good condition by its workforce.

top left:
The darkened area of Attercliffe is Brown Bayley's

top right:
The Brown Bayley offices on the right and the Friends and Adult school on the left

middle:
Stuart, second left, with friends on a Brown Bayley's reunion

bottom:
Looking over Coleridge Road bridge on to the goods yard at Brown Bayley Photographs: Stuart Green

Everyone, hopefully, knows that Sir Christopher Wren built St. Paul's Cathedral. Visitors to the cathedral can read on his tomb - "If you seek Wren's monument look around you", but it does not tell them that Brown Bayley did a very interesting job in keeping St Pauls intact. The famous dome is supported by eight massive piers, but the loading is such that there is always a tendency to push them outwards. The drum of the dome expands in hot weather, but masonry on its own does not contract again in cold weather. So the condition develops to the stage that, if nothing were done about it, the whole structure would eventually collapse. Stainless steel chains were fitted to overcome this weakness. These were made of 'Twoscore" steel, the first was supplied in 1930, the photo on this page show what it looked like. There were in all thirty articulations (or links). Each link of the chain was about 16 ft. in length, making a total for the chain of 450 feet and the weight of the complete chain was just under 30. Tons this was placed at a point on the dome, just below the Whispering Gallery, where the outside diameter is about 140 feet, and, by means of wedges, a stress of approximately 1000 tons was imposed on the chain.

A second chain was supplied in 1931. This was of a similar construction to the first, but of a greater length, although the overall weight was less. It is situated 150 feet lower down in the dome structure

But to return to the story of the first chain, it is remembered that the firm's fleet of steam wagons took it all the way from Leeds Road, Attercliffe to London.

The links which straddle St Paul's Cathedral Dome. Photograph: Stuart Green

The Attercliffe Palace

In 1955 when the Palace closed its doors for the very last time I was only seven but I remember the buzz outside the place when the final show was finished.

Cyril Lymer removed all the seating from the Palace and I am reliably informed by his son, John, (a good friend), he then sold 'em on at a bob a time. Nice one Cyril!

Stuart Green, as I mentioned earlier supplied me with some marvellous information and photographs of the area in and around Brown Bayleys. He also supplied the photographs below of the Brown Bayleys amateur dramatics society in a production of A Country Girl.

The menu card was signed by all the players on the reverse, including Harry Brearley.

above right : The Attercliffe Palace

below left: The Complimentary Dinner card

below right: The back of the dinner card signed by all the players.

Palace

After a modicum of success in Northampton with the Empire Music Hall, Frank MacNaughten got the idea that a suburban music hall would do well in Sheffield. He floated a company in 1897 with a capital of £10,000 to build a hall in the populous suburb of Attercliffe. One of the directors was Fred Lawton, of a firm of solicitors, Hardy, Lawton and Company of Sheffield.

The Alhambra opened on the 3rd January, 1898. Unfortunately, the Alhambra was not the success hoped for, although it did improve as time went on. In 1907 it was sold to T. Allan Edwards of Derby, who changed its name to the Palace. It was run as a music hall until 1913 and then finally changed to a cinema. Years later it made a return to greatness as a music hall in the boom period following the second war.

above: The Chorus Line for Country Girl

bottom: All the players taking a curtain call for their production of a Country Girl

Palais de Danse

Derek Deacon, ex Attercliffe, now of Tintwistle, Glossop, lived above the old Benefit Shoe shop on Attercliffe Road. Derek as well as a few members of his family helped out at the Palais de Danse in the forties and fifties. The price for the hire of skates in 1948 was 1/6d. The opening time was 7pm until 10.30pm. The owners at that time were a Mr Travis and Mr Jeffcock.

Derek also remembers the snooker hall above Boots the Chemist, just across the road from his home, on the corner of Worksop Road. A place his mother was not all that keen on him frequenting. He states that the hall had two entrances and he could keep a watchful eye out for his mother coming across the road and up the stair at the front whilst he exited by the rear, deceptive but effective.

left:
The old building that on the upper floor once housed the Snooker Hall.

below:
The exterior and interior of the Palais de Danse
Photo Derek Deakin

Gem Stores - George E Murat

The Gem Stores (George E Murat, hence GEM stores) on Attercliffe Road was one of my favourite shops - toys, models, cycles, lead soldiers and many more items a kid could while away a couple of hours playing with. This shop was run by George Murat, a kindly man, who always seemed to have time to talk to me, a small child. Whether good businessman or genuine snotty nosed kid lover, it didn't really make any difference to me, he seemed interested and that's all that counts to a customer - today's shop assistants please note. From my first memories of Attercliffe, GEM stores was just there, as much a cornerstone of Attercliffe to me as was Banners to most people.

George Murat, sadly, passed away quite recently - he spent the last few years of his life in the Upperthorpe area. I received the pictures you see below from his daughter Christine and son in law George Mottram, who live in Cumbria. They both originally lived in Attercliffe and went to Huntsmans Garden School. George's mother, Emmie Mottram, worked at Wagstaffs sweet shop as did my own mother, Joan Liversidge, although not at the same time. George Mottram was brought up in Bodmin Street in the next yard to the former Member of Parliament Joe Ashton.

above:
George Murat with one of his great grandchildren

left:
A photograph of the Gem Stores after its closure. Mr Murat can just be seen reflected in the window actually taking the photo.

Photographs:
George and Christine Mottram

Ernest Wagstaff

Ernest Wagstaff kept a shop on Attercliffe for over 30 years. His sweet and tobacco shop at 841 Attercliffe Road was the normal stop off point for anyone visiting the Globe or Adelphi picture houses. The foyer of the Globe and Adelphi were not adorned with drink and sweet selections as cinemas are today. So a visit to stock up on your fags or sweets was a must and Ernest always stayed open until after the last admissions. My mother, as stated previously, worked at the toffee tin and so did my aunt, Glennis Renshaw (née Otley).

For a number of years in the late 40s and early 50s, Nellie Wagstaff (Ernest's first wife) ran a hairdressing business from the back of the sweetshop premises.

left:
Ernest Wagstaff in his shop.
Photograph: Iris Wagstaff

middle:
The shop in its last few months.
My mother peering out of the door.
Photograph: Iris Wagstaff

below:
A dinner of local traders:
left to right Ernest Wagstaff, George Murat, John Thompson, John Allen, John Cutler, both Mr Thompson and Mr Cutler were employees of Mr Allen. The three ladies are Edith Allen (George Murats sister), Christiana Murat (George's wife) and Nellie Wagstaff, (Ernest first wife). The Allens had cycle shops on Infirmary Road and at Firth Park.
Photograph: Christine and George Mottram

Banners

Banners was the shop for Attercliffe people - if you had the cash. It was a great shop and even if you didn't have the money you could still get your goods here. They took your loan cheques and credit notes from money lenders and gave you your change in Banners Money. It was a ploy that worked because you couldn't go anywhere else with that money so you were obviously tied to trade with Banners.

To this day the John Banners building is still the beacon of Attercliffe. There was another John Banners shop at Fir Vale,

John Banner himself lived at Chippingham House around the time of the First World War.

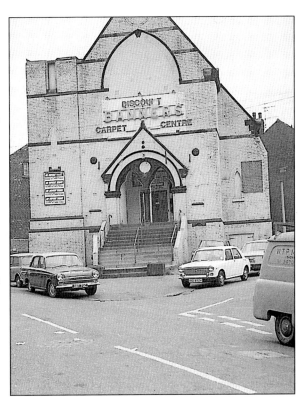

above: Banner carpet centre Chippingham Place - used to be an old methodist chapel

left and below:
Banners escalator, the first one to be installed in a department store outside of London.

left:
John Banners

below:
Banner Money
metal

bottom:
Looking down attercliffe
from outside Banners

top: Attercliffe early evening

left:
Banners Money - plastic

below: John Banners, Shortridge Street, and Ernest Burgess

above:
John Banners building now houses an antique and collector's floor

below:
Banners closing down sale

Reverend Hone giving one of his usual rousing speeches from the back of a Robert Earl and Sons Lorry

Looking down Broughton Lane on to Attercliffe Common and Milford Street

The Friendship on Tinsley Park Road

At the junction of Broughton Lane with Tinsley Park Road. Cuddy Meadows in the distance

Jodies Snacks - old chocolate shop and horse and jockey pub. I recall these shops as a tripe shop and herbalists.

The barges are now more for the tourist or wildlife observer than for hauling coal.

Carbrook Conservative Club before its demolition and subsequent rebirth on Broughton Lane in the old Bird in Hand premises.

Looking towards the end of Attercliffe Common with the AEI on the right and in the distance the Commercial Hotel.

The Staniforth Road doorway on Shentons furniture shop, which, obviously used to be a Montague Burtons Tailors.

The Masterchef Butchers and a Swap Shop at the bottom of Staniforth Road

Leeds Road around the 1930s

The New Inn on Carbrook Street

The petrol station, Emmanuel Church
and on the right hand side of the picture: Carters manufacturing chemist - of Carters Little Liver Pills fame

The boarded up premises is now a sex shop but in the late fifties there was a public house situated here, The Victoria Inn - no picture of this premises can be found. Baker Street and Frankern Motors can be seen on right.

The boats on the canal are now pleasure cruisers and the buildings in the background are no longer the dark steel firms but large sports stadia

Looking up Attercliffe Common from the bottom of Belmoor Road.

Jessop Saville Ltd, Brightside Lane in decline

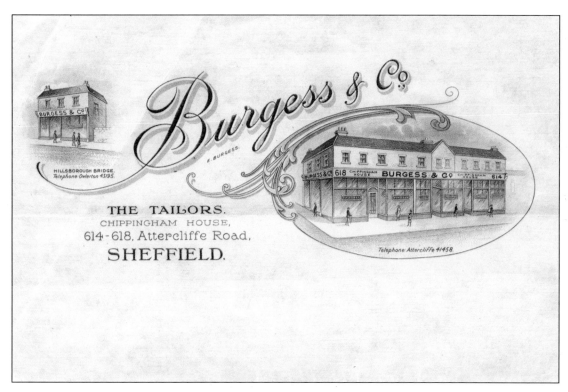

A Burgess and Co Letterhead supplied by Mr Derek Croft-Smith

Wagstaff Sweet Shop, Attercliffe Road.

Jonas Colvers on Birch Road

Looking from Broughton Lane, the railway lines on the left and the canal, with barge heading for Sheffield to the right indicate a variety of transport came through Attercliffe, to the left is were the Attercliffe Centretainments is now situated.

above: George Oxleys on Attercliffe Road - now Harratts Car Showrooms

right: Advertisement which appeared in Local Directory in 1963 for Oxleys

The Broughton Pub can just be seen on the left of picture with Goulden Place and a few of the business on Attercliffe Common. As you can see this picture was taken in 1984 when Attercliffe was succumbing to the steel closures.

The Salutation, and the Pavilion

Looking down Attercliffe Common. The picture was taken in the 1960s from the top of Bradford Street and captures Berkley Road, Belmoor Road as well as a few of the local businesses. Looming in the background Carbrook Elementary School

by Gary Mackender

attercliffe -
another wander up the 'cliffe

a painting by M Rick

63

a painting by T Byrne

Matthews Furniture shop on the corner of Attercliffe Common and Brinsworth Street.

The Vestry Hall, Attercliffe Common

Rather than going to your doctor, Raymond Hall's shop on Staniforth Road would be visited for a discussion about your ailment, and generally, it has to be said, a remedy was more often than not given.

Tommy Wards at the end of Attercliffe Road

*Looking on to Attercliffe Road
from outside Fred Mellings
printers on Zion Lane*

Coleridge Road School - happy days?

W Pierrepoint's premises seems to have been derelict for an age.

Another monument to a Montague Burton shop - this time on the corner of Vicarage Road

A Fair in Attercliffe, possibly Coleridge Road (but I don't honestly recall any three storey houses in that area)

Brown Bayleys ready for demolition in August 1985

Brown Bayleys being demolished in August 1985

left to right: My father, Joe Liversidge, with his brothers Harry and John in an Attercliffe pub in the fifties.

Attercliffe roofscape 1975

A rather spooky shot of the interior of Hilltop Chapel

Late fifties, the volume of traffic on the roads seems almost sedate compared to today's hustle.

*Carlton House
from the rear and side
and top picture a view from the
front*

left:
Spear and
Jacksons, Norfolk
Bridge, being
demolished in
1985

below:
Spartan Steel

The Interior of the Most Haunted pub in Sheffield, if not England! The Carbrook Hall

Meg's Cafe on the junction of Brompton Road, Newhall Road and Attercliffe Common

Attercliffe Pubs

Attercliffe boasted a wealth of public houses and working men's clubs along its thoroughfare. From Weedon Street to Tommy Wards (with only slight detours) you could enter the portals of more than 50 pubs. Some pub crawl that would be.

Commercial

The **Commercial** which seemed to be looming at the end of Weedon Street forever is now, as I write, being demolished. The **Union** and the **Royal** went in the Seventies. The **Burns** met its demise earlier in the 60s and the **Tinsley Hotel** went out of business a little later in the early seventies. The **Royal** was possibly previously named the **Attercliffe Arms or Inn** and could have also been named the **Crown Inn** and was then at the address of 623 Attercliffe Road on the corner of Blucher Street. This, I think, then changed into a lodging house, before reverting back to a pub.

Royal Hotel

Slightly off the Cliffe, Carbrook Street had **The New Inn, White Lion, British Oak** and the **Excelsior** which was situated at the top of Carbrook Street at it joining with Attercliffe Common. Also in that small area there was the **Industry** on Dunlop Street. All of these pubs are no more.

Interior of the Carbrook Hall

Also in this area and still serving beer are the **Carbrook Hall** and the **Pheasant (Stumble Inn)** both of which seem to do very well especially the **Carbrook Hall** which has marketed itself excellently and which boasts a lovely beer/food garden. Just off Attercliffe was the **Yellow Lion** on Clifton Street, supposedly

workmen in 1890, whilst digging some footing at the side of this pub came across the base of the gibbet which had been used for the ghastly imprisonment of Spence Broughton's skeleton.

above:
New Inn, Carbrook Street

left:
The Pheasant from Bee Street

After Carbrook Street the next pub on Attercliffe Common was the **Broughton** which was closed and then demolished in the mid eighties and stood where we now park our cars when we call to the arena. Across the road from where this pub stood, Whitbreads have invested a large sum of money and built the **Arena Square** which is very popular with families having their meals before heading into the centretainments complex.

Broughton Inn awaiting demolition

Just off the 'Cliffe was Milford Street which housed two pubs, the **Fitzwilliam** and the **Wentworth** (which is still thriving at the time of going to press).

Broughton Lane not only boasted the **Broughton** at its corner with Attercliffe Common but the **Enfield, Railway (Noose and Gibbet)** and the **Bird in Hand**. Also just around the top corner on to Tinsley Park Road was the **Friendship** and **Fishermans.** All of these premises still stand except for the **Fishermans** which was closed and demolished in the seventies and the Bird in Hand has now become the Carbrook Conservative Club.

Fitzwilliam

Back on to Attercliffe Common and the **Lambpool** is next standing at the corner of Attercliffe and Janson Street. Head down Janson Street to Hawke Street (don't ask me why the road changes names) you cross Abyssinia Bridge and come to the **Wellington** another now departed building.

Carbrook Conservative Club bar, previously the Bird in Hand

One dinner time in the mid sixties I was surprised how empty it was when three of us entered and asked for three pints and three pie and peas. The lady behind the bar said "hurry up and take three and sit down". She was pulling copious amounts of beer into what seemed to be every glass in the establishment and after

The Wellington on the corner Brightside Lane and Hawke St

about five minutes she had lined up about 100 pints on the bar.

Whoosh, the doors flew open and the men just grabbed a pint or more off the bar and scuttled off to a seat. Food was ordered, but not much and the ladies who now numbered about five behind the bar just kept pulling pints. After about 20 minutes it emptied and I can honestly say I never saw anyone pay for a drink. I have heard from some old steelmen that the ladies used to go around the tables with a clippies bag and count the glasses and collect the money owed. Very trusting.

The **Filesmiths** and the **Amberley** almost next to each other came next before somewhat of a gap - about 100 yards to the next pub the **Salutation** on the corner with Coleridge Road. **The Gate Inn,** to my recollection not the most upmarket pub on the 'Cliffe and the **Hill Top** came on the bend of Attercliffe Common just before its connection to Attercliffe Road. The first pub on Attercliffe Road was the **Tramcar** followed quickly by the **Golden Ball** or the Gilded Knacker as it was locally known.

On Newhall Road there was the **Vine, Brickmakers, Lodge, Forge** all long since ceased as licensed premise. Also there was a snooker hall. I cannot recall if this was a licensed premises or not.

Back on Attercliffe the **Greyhound**, which still stands and seems to be thriving at the moment is next and the **Travellers** (run by Sheffield Wednesday and England Centre Half, Peter Swan in the sixties) is just before Worksop Road. The Travellers had stood empty now for quite some period, hopefully it can be opened as another of the Camra pubs or some enterprising brewery might give it another try.

Amberley Hotel and Filesmiths on the corner of Tuxford Road

Salutation Inn

The Gate Inn

The Greyhound, with its old tiles still on show

On the corner of Worksop Road was the Omnibus with its large concert room and distinctive yellowish tiles. On Worksop Road itself there were four pubs the **Britannia**, which had associations with Benjeman Huntsman, **The Cocked Hat, The Cutlers, Old Blue Bell** and the **White Hart**. Once again all these premises are still standing but only two are still continuing as public houses, the **Cocked Hat** and **Cutlers (now Farrahs).**

The Coach and Horses

Around the corner and back on to Attercliffe Road we come to the **Coach and Horses** which was originally named the **Barrel** and was built in 1819, it changed its name to the **Coach and Horses** when the stage coaches started passing in 1838. The pub was rebuilt in 1901 and closed in the late seventies as a pub but is now resurrected as the Swan Hotel.

The White Hart, Worksop Road

Across the road is the **King's Arms** and facing this is the **Station Hotel** both of which are still trying their best to beat the drastic recession that hit this area. The **Queen's Head** was next on the corner of Shirland Land, a large Tennants pub whose frame is still standing but has not served beer for many years. On Shirland lane itself is the **Fox House.**

The Queens Head

Back on to Attercliffe Road and the next pub, the **Victoria Inn** which stood on the corner of Sleaford Street is a mystery to myself in that I cannot find a picture of this establishment after about 10 years of searching. The **Victoria** and the **Tinsley Hotel** are the only two pubs I cannot find any pictorial reference to anywhere, after many year trying.

The Fox House on Shirland Lane

79

The **Horse and Jockey** is the next pub on the walk up Attercliffe and is not only still going but has just had an expensive refit. Give it a visit and see what you think.

The **Dog and Partridge** at the present time is being worked on to make it into a lap dancing venue. Somehow, I don't think you'll be getting a pint in there for £-/1/10^d, like I did on my first visit.

The **Carlton**, facing the bottom of Staniforth Road is next and is now on the list of CAMRA pubs in Sheffield. Across the road is the **Robin Hood** now a wife swopping venue, Le Chambre. What fun!

The **Sportsman**, previously a Wards pub, was named the **Indigo** for a while. I think it was a gay bar as is/was the next pub the **Bulldog,** now called the Bar Celona or something equally exotic. In between the Sportsman and the Bulldog is the **Dancing Dollar Club** this is now a lap dancing club and formerly used to be the **Attercliffe Non Political Club.**

The next public house after the old bulldog was the **Washford Arms** at Washford Bridge, then the **Norfolk Arms** which stood in the shadow of the Tempered Springs, just before Norfolk Bridge.

You wouldn't think that just a hundred yard walk from the Norfolk Arms and you could be in the **North Pole**, well the **North Pole Inn** on Sussex Street.

Back on to the last stretch of Attercliffe and the only pub I remember in situ on this stretch was the **Twelve O'Clock** directly facing Tommy Wards. This pub closed in the 60s and its licence was transferred to the **High Noon**, in the Woodthorpe area of Sheffield.

Green Dragon, Attercliffe Road

Sportsman, Attercliffe Road, previously the Hope & Anchor

Bulldog, Attercliffe Road at Washford Bridge

Norfolk Arms, Attercliffe Road at Norfolk Bridge

The Alexandra Hotel, on Carlisle Street just of Newhall Road

Hill Top Hotel, Attercliffe Common

Brickmakers Arms on Newhall Road

Cocked Hat on Worksop Road

Horse and Jockey, Attercliffe Road

Wentworth Hotel, Milford Street

Washford Arms, Attercliffe Road, Washford Bridge

Dog and Partridge, Attercliffe Road

Effigy of Spence Broughton outside the Noose and Gibbet

Kings Head on Attercliffe Road

The Carlton on Attercliffe Road

Lambpool on Attercliffe Common

Enfield and Railway on Broughton Lane

Tramcar, Attercliffe Road

Players Cafe, old Carbrook School, Attercliffe Common

Cutlers Arms, Worksop Road

Golden Ball, Attercliffe Road at the intersection with Old Hall Road and Leeds Road.

The Twelve O'Clock pub sited at the beginning of Attercliffe Road. The picture was taken from the top of T W Wards
Photo Ms Catlin

Continuing, only slightly, past the end of Attercliffe Road is the Hole in the Wall, previously known as the Wicker Brewery which was situated just before the Wicker Arches.

A Family (Friends and Neighbours) Album

A few photographs of members of my family and friends who lived in Attercliffe.....

right:
My Grandfather second from right on back row ready for a game of cricket

right centre:
Richard Otley, my grandfather in his bus conductor's uniform

below:
Glennis Otley, my mother's sister with a friend, Linda Barrett who lived a few houses away on Belmoor Road.

above:
My father and grandfather in 32 Belmoor Road

left:
Joan Liversidge, my mother pushing me on the swings

right:
On the back of the motorcycle is Tommy Smith, a neighbour who lived at number 28 Belmoor Road. The other chap is unknown to me.

below middle:
A very early photograph of Mrs Wheeler, a neighbour, who lived at number 34 Belmoor Road, on a mode of transport that I have not seen the like of before

below: Mr and Mrs Ramsden of 30 Belmoor Road with my mother, Joan in 1930

below: Paul Smedley and myself

above: An Attercliffe day out at Brid. Lee Froggatt (what is he wearing?), Allan Dent, Fred Needham and Michael Liversidge in front of their Cortina and Morris Traveller.
Lee lived on Amberley Street, Allan on Bradford Street, Fred on Bold Street

below: Lee Froggatt (without the silly headgear) showing off his catch

below:
Janet Green lived a few doors away at number 36 Belmoor Road

above:
My cousins, Brian, taking a beating, and David, his brother

above:
Brian and David sat on my shoulders

below:
Paul Smedley carrying me around

below:
Janet Green and Iris Taylor in the rec

As you can see from the above photographs, the background has become equally as noteworthy as the families or friends depicted on them. Janet and Iris are stood in front of the Carbrook Recreation ground play area, swings etc and the clinic is just visible behind Janet's head.

The other three pictures detail Brown Bayleys in the background. The extension being built on one photo and complete on the other two. These pictures also show the back to back housing and outside loos we used.

Postcards of old attercliffe

Being a collector of postcards I find such elation from finding cards of Sheffield and especially Attercliffe. I found these cards as far afield as Jersey, London, Newcastle, the Isle of Wight, Birmingham and some at the odd car boot sale.

The Cammell Laird series of Postcards is I think a set of eight as you can see I'm one short.

Postcards of old attercliffe

Old public houses of Attercliffe on postcards are fairly hard to come by these days, so as you can see I do not have a vast collection of them.

The Pheasant Inn , Old Building

The Excelsior before demolition

The Carbrook Hall

The Alexandra Hotel - Carlisle Street

The Lambpool

The Norfolk Arms

Postcards of old attercliffe

General views of Attercliffe: The Cottages at Attercliffe, Brook Cottages, Albert Taylor, wholesale shop postcard advert, a view of Attercliffe Road, Attercliffe Church, and Carbrook Church which was on Attercliffe Common.

Some of the local businesses who were trading in and around the Attercliffe area in the 1960.
Some of these companies are still trading today

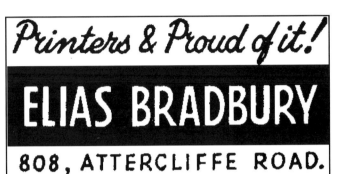
Bradburys was my first employer as an apprentice compositor in the printing industry

attercliffe - *another wander up the 'cliffe*

from a 1963 Local Directory

Attercliffe Road
odd numbers
Twelve O'Clock Street
Greystock Street

Sutherland Street
Princess Street

173	Taylor John Dunford& Co	
181	Moorwood	Hairdresser
183	Turner	Shopkeeper
197	Walton	Shopkeeper
199	Royds Post & M. O. Office	
203	Storide Ltd.	Gas distributors
209	Halfway Cafe	
211	Spruce Dry Cleaners	
215	Blue Star Garage	

Royds Mill Street

Carter & Sons Ltd. Mfng. Chemists

Windsor Street

Fowler Ltd. Don Foundry

Attercliffe Bridge

375-383	Brown Ltd	Laboratory Furnishers

Washford Road

387	Bulldog P.H	
401	Clarke & Sons Ltd	Ironfounders

Trent Street

421	Fox	Wardrobe dlr.
423	Smith	Newsagents
425	Squires	Shopkeeper
427	Hallewell	Turf commsssn. agt
429	Lawler	Boot Reprairer
431	Littlewood	Fishing tackle dlr
433	Smith	Wardrobe Dealer
435	Nichols	Hairdresser

Stevenson Road

437	Fergione	Beer Retailer
439	Gloria's, baby linen shop	
441	Wilkinson	Fried Fish Dealer
443	Barbara, Ladies' Hairdresser	
445	Artificial Teeth Repair Co. Dental Technicians	
451	Cheung	Laundry

Armstead Road

453	Beaumont & Moseley	Shopkeeper
455	Proctor	Shopkeeper
457	Hardy	Baker
459	Broughton	Tobacconist
461	Ross	Shokeeper
463 / 465	B & J Plant	Plumbers

Baldwin Street

471	Green Dragon	Public House
507/515	B & J Plant	Plumbers

Heppenstall Lane

533	Wigfall & Son	Cycle Dlrs.
537-543	Senior	Clothiers
543	Instant Watch Co.	Jewellers
545	British Relay Wireless	Television relay.
547	Snacks Buffet Bar	
549	Maison Daveen	Ladies Hairdrs

Kimberley Street

551	Boldock	Fish Monger
553	Billingham	Tobacconist
555	Bradbury Jn.	Who. Statnr
557	Gallons Ltd	Provision Dlrs.
559	Willerby & Co. Ltd.	Tailors
561	Senior Electronic Service Ltd. Radio Engnrs.	
563	Carlton	Public House

Oakes Green

575	Dog & Partridge	Public House
579	Benson	Hosiery Specialist
581	Melias Ltd.	Provsn. Dlrs.
583	Needham	Pork butcher
585	Combes	Shoe repars
587	Diane's	Fancy Goods Retailers
589	Downs & Sons	Butchers
591-597	Wades Furnishing Stores Ltd. House Furnishers	

Colwall Street

599	Martins	Dyers & Cleaners
601	Domestic Electric Rentals Television rentals	
603	Burton	M. P. S. Chemist
605	Blaskeys	Wallpaper dlrs
609	Oliver	Butcher
611	Schweitzer & Sons	Furniture Dlrs.
613	Greenlees & Sons Easiephit Footwear Ltd	Boot Makers
615-617	Halford Cycle & Co.	Cycle Agts. & Dlrs.
619	Pell	Tailor

Sleaford Street

621a	Isherwoods	Electrical dlrs
623	Brighter Homes Ashley United	
Industries Ltd	Wallpaper Mfrs.	
625	Reed	Tailor
627	Hukin	Butcher
629	Midland Bank Ltd	

Baker Street

641-649	Brightside & Carbrook Co-operative Society	

Zion Lane

663	Johnson Bros.	Dyers & Cleaners
665-667	Senior Percy Ltd	Boot & Shoe Dlrs.
671	Neales Ltd.	Costumiers
673	Cass Leslie	Retail Jeweller
675	Walkers	Shoe shop
677	Hipps	Tailors
679 -683	Woolworth	Bazaar
685	Collier	Tailors
687	Cox Radiovison Ltd.	
689	Stylo Boot Co. Ltd.	
693	Nu-vu Rentals Television Dlrs	
699-701	Betty	Costumiers
703-705	Naylor	Retailer Jeweller
707	Meadow Dairy	Butter Dlrs
709	King's Head	Public House
715-717	Benefit Footwear Ltd.	
719	Reed, Neville	Tailors

721	Yeomans Jr.	Who. Tobacconist

Church Lane

	Christ Church	
	Christ Church Sunday School	
747	Williams Deacon's Bank Ltd.	
753	Pierrepont	Greengrocer
759	Singer Sewing Machine Co. Ltd.	
761	Snelson's	Radio Supplies Dlrs.
763-765	Barclays bank ltd.	
773	General plumbers and Glaziers Ltd	
775	Reed	Tailors
777	Rose	Outfitter
779	Boston Shoe Co.	Boot & Shoe Dlrs.
781	Melias	Provision Dlrs.
783-787	Ministry of Pensions & National Insurance	

Vicarage Road

799	Kitter	Ladies outfitter
801	Brightside & Carbrook Co-op Chemists	
803	Taylor & Co.	Who. Tobacconists
805	Althams Stores	Tea Merch.
807	Morris	Paint Merch.
809	Quick Press Ltd.	Cleaners

Brompton Road

813-815	Brompton Snack Bar & Cafe	
817-819	Gibbs & Ward	Wollen Mers
821	Gallons	Provision Dlrs.
823	Shaw	Butcher
825	Cook Olive	Draper
827	Domestic Hardware Stores & Ironmongers	
829	Harris	Grocer
831	Marshall	Leather Fctrs
833	Caravan Supplies, hardwear dlrs	
835	Fragrance	Cleaners
837	Whittaker	Florist
839	Cooke	Fishmngr.
841	Wagstaff	Shopkeeper
843	Hammonds	Shopkeeper
845	Curson	Draper
847	Oliver	Butcher
849	Newsom	Gents' Outfitter

Clay Street

851	Tram Car Inn	Public House
853	Woodrow	Butcher
857	Harris	Confectioners
859	Pierrepont	Greengrocer
861	Hudson & Sons	Hardware dlrs
863	Post & M.O. Office	
865	Fairprice Fireplace	Fireplace Mfrs.

Attercliffe Road

even numbers

	Oxley & Sons	Vulcan Foundry
54	Wolstenholme & Sons Ltd.	Welders
70	Bentley Brothers Ltd	
		Motor Body Builders
72-76	Bentley Brothers Ltd. Commercial Vehicle Repairs	
94	The Furnival Steel Co. Ltd.	
96	Sheffield Metallurgical Laboratories	
108	Footit & Whatley	Shopfitters

Warren Street

160	Norfolk Arms	Public House
	Tempered Springs Co Ltd.	
180/186	Wincott Ltd	Furnace Builders
	Andrews & Co (Royds Works)	
		Steel Manufacturers
	Hardenite Steel Co. Ltd. (Hardenite Steel Works)	
		Steel Manufacturers
	Dyson Ltd	Ganister Manifacturers
262	Blue Star Garage. Ltd. National Coal Board	
270	Thompson Machine Tools Ltd.	
286	Beeley Foundry	Light Castings Ltd.
	Iron Founders	
286	Metal Heat Treatment Ltd.	
	Heat Treatment Specialists	
	Emmanuel Church	
286	Wizard Adrasives Ltd	
286	Steelbuffs Ltd abrasive materials mfrs.	
292	Carbolite co.Labroatory equipment supplies	
296-298	Kennings Ltd. Motor Spirit Service Stn	

Don Terrace

380	Washford Arms	Public House
396	Smith	Grocer
400	Attercliffe Tyre Co. Ltd.	

Lovetot Road

436	Hookham Ltd. Motor Haulage Contrs	
436	Pigott	Engineer
442	Attercliffe Road Christian Spiritualist Mission	
444	Wilson	Herbalists

Effingham Road

482	Pickford Holland & Co Refactory goods mnfs	
482	Effco Furnaces Ltd. Heat Treatment specialists	
504	Sportsman Inn	
	Spartan Steel & Alloys Ltd	Steel mfrs
542	Pearce	Fried fish dlr
544	Samuels & Sons	Credit Drapers
546	Beldam Asbestos Co. Ltd.	
546	Auto Klean Strainers Ltd.	
548	Robin Hood	Public House
	Robin Hood Yard	
		Heselwood W. Iron & Steel Mer.
566-568	Hartley & Son Ltd	Printers
566-568	Hartley Marsland Ltd. Office furnishers	
570	The Sheffield Savings Bank	

580	Yorkshire Penny Bank Ltd.	

Staniforth Road

582	Burton Montague Ltd.	Tailors
590	Timpson Ltd.	Boot & Shoe Dlrs.
592	Hopkinsons Ltd	Grocers
594	Dutfield	Fruitrs
596	Timpson Ltd	Boot & Shoe Dlrs
596a	Admirality Contract & Purchase Dept	
596a	Ministry of Public Buildings and Works	
598	Vickers	Chemist
600	Hodgkinson	Shopkpr
602-608	Littlewoods Stores	
614-618	Burgess Ltd.	Tailors

Chippenham Place

620-636	John Banner Ltd	
	Drapers & General-House Furnishers	

Baltic Road

638	Horse & Jockey	Public House
642	Bullimore	Herbalist
644	Lee's	Tripe Dressers

Baltic Lane

648	Scott Jn.	Hairdresser
650/652	Talbot	Butcher
656	Westminster Bank	

Shirland Lane

660	Queens Head	Public house
662	Leeson	Newsagents
674/676	Fine Fare Supermarket	
678	Jacqueline, ladies costumes	
680	Brook Shaw. Ltd.	
682	Slack Dennis A. Ltd.	Bakers
684	Hattons	Butchers
686	Hyman's	Turf Commision agt
688	Brightside Carbrook	
	Painting &.Decorating Depot	

Brinsworth Street

694	Matthews Furnishers Ltd	
698	Styan	Bakers
700	Wiley & Co. Ltd.	Wine & Spirit Mers
702	Levison	Drapers
706	Stamp	Confectioners
706a	King Coal & Co.	Coal Mers
708	Clethro	Fried Fish Dlrs
710	Ricky	Costumiers
712	Martins Ltd.	Dyers & Cleaners
714	Horswood H. & E. Ltd	Catering Serv
716	Modes E. & B.	Costumiers

Bodmin Street

718-724	Freeda	Furnisher
726	Myers	Butchers
728	Hewitt Harry	Hairdressers
730	New Cake shop, bakers	
732	Station Hotel	Public House
736	Radio Rentals. Ltd.	
738	Curry's	Radio & television dlrs
754	Foggitt Cecil M., M.B., B. Ch.	
754	Wallis	Physcn & surgn
756	Coach & Horses	Public House

760	Sheffield Billiards Halls Co. Ltd.	
762	Dobson's	Television/Radio Supplies
764	Boots	Chemists

Worksop Road

776	O'Neill	Ladies' Hairdresser
778	Thompson	Cafe
784	Travellers' Inn	Public House
786	Pickering	Tripe Dlr.
788	Lily Law	Shopkeeper
790	Colligan	Hairdresser

Beverley Street

792-794	Liberal Club & Institute Ltd.	
796	Jarman	Retail Jeweller
798-800	Coombes & Co.	Boot Repairers
802	Don Valley Cleaners Ltd.	
804	Kirk	Fishmngrs
806	Beaumont	Electrical Contractors
808	Bradbury Elias	Printers
822	Greyhound Inn	Public House
824-826	Sheffield Corp Public Baths	

Oldhall Road

838	Golden Ball	Public House
862-864	Gilles Ernest	Optician
866-868	Said	Cafe
870-872	Attercliffe Sale & Exchange	

Attercliffe Common

odd numbers

3-15	Brightside & Carbrook	
	Co-operative Society Ltd.	
17	Globe Service Station	
39	Blyth Jas.	Physcn. & Surgeon
39	Blyth Kenneth	Physcn. & Surgeon
	Attercliffe Vestry Hall	
	Community Centre	
	Womens Welfare Clinic	
51	Ministry of Labour & National	
	Service Employment Exchange	
51	Tudor Autos	Motor Car Body Bldrs
59	Hunt	Dairyman
61	Ismail - Jama	Dining Rooms

Newark Street

65	Hill Top Hotel	Public house
69-71	Victoria Wine Co	
73	Dean Brothers	Grocers
75	Welbon & Sons	Fishing Tackle Dlrs
77	Needham	Fried Fish Dlr.
79	Gowers & Son Ltd.	Grocers

Frank Place

	Old Burial Ground	
127	Nuttall	Sports Outfitter
131	Allen	Chemists
133	Wilks	Butcher
135	Attercliffe Sales & Exchange Dlrs.	

Leigh Street

137	Kirkup	Hardware dlrs.
139-141	Stone W	Greengrocer
143	Nur Bros	Ladies Outfitters

145	National Provincial Bank Ltd.	

Rotherham Street

161	March The Tailor	
163	Quick Press	Dyers & Cleaners
165	Boldock	Fishmonger
169	Baker	Ironmonger

Bradford Street

171	Cain	Beer Retailer
173	Waterall	Pork Butchers
175	Oliver & Sons	Butchers
177	Zindani	Butcher
179	Martins Ltd.	Dyers & Cleaners
181	Laming	Baker

Steadfast Street

183 / 187	Carbrook Motors - Dyson Motors	
		Motor Car Dealers
189-195	Brightside & Carbrook	
	Co-operative Society Ltd	
191	South Yorkshire District Co-operative	
	Laundries Assoociation Ltd	

Berkley Street

201	Benxix	Launderette
203	Savage & Sons	Musical Dlrs.
205	Dinitto	Jewellers
207	Langton & Sons Ltd.	Boot Mfrs.
209	Travis	Draper
211	Wagstaff	Woodworkers supplies
213	Dewhurst	Butchers
215	Hughes	Fruitr.

Amberley Street

221	Amberley Hotel	Public House
227	Peacock	Confetnr.

Tuxford Road

229	File Smiths' Arms	Public House
237	Cutts, Frank	Turf Commision agt
239	Harry marks & Co.	Outfitters
241	The Pet Shop	
243	Carbrook Cabinet & Co. Ltd.	
		House Furnishers
255/257	Spencers	Wallpaper Dlr.
259	Falkner	Drapers
263	Dobson	Physcn. & Surgn.
271	Simmonite	Haulage Contractors
273	Middleton	Tobacconist
277-283	Riley Jnr. & Son. Ltd.	
		Electrical Accessories Dlrs.
287-289	Taylor	Grocer

Janson Street

291	Lambpool Hotel	Public House
297	Booth	Newsagents
309/311	Premier Snack Bar	Shopkeeper
313	Matthewman	Fruitr
315	Webster	Hardware dlr
317	Brawn	Cafe
319	Factory Painters	store
319	Gow Safe Board Ltd.	Store
321	Newsam	Ladies' Hairdressers
323-325	N. C. F. Ltd.	Fish mers.

331	Annes	Drapers
333	Harry's	Hairdressers
337	Carbrook Working Mens'	
	Conservative Club	
349	Carbrook Post & M. O. Office	
349	Barnard	Stationr
351	Pashley	Draper
353	Khyber Cafe	
367	Pitcher	Draper
375	Hartley	Tool Dlrs.
379	Gill	Butchers
381	Greensmith	Provision Dlr.
383	Marvel	Dyers & Cleaner
385-387	Hallatt	Chemists
389	Roddis	Refreshment Rooms

Milford Street

391	Thompson Jnr.	Fruitiers
395	Snart	Draper
397	Ariston (Revett & Co.)Ltd	
		Tobacconists
399	Tracy	Turf Commision Agt
401	Johnson	Grocers
405	Randall & Wagstaff	Newsagents
407	Clark	Electronic engr
409	Bladen	Dressmakers
411	Hudson	Hardware Dlrs.
413	Websters	Boot Repairers
415	My Fair Lady	Hairdressers
419	Stamford	Fishing Tackle
421	Mann	Pork Butchers
423-433	Shaw & Son Ltd.	Outfitters
435	Lant	Fried Fish Dlrs.
437	Yeomans Jnr.	
		Wholesale Tobacconist
439-441	Reliance Transport electrical service Ltd	

Carbrook Street

443	Fearn & Son	Motor engnrs
453	Dobson Ltd.	General Dlrs.
455	Jacksons	Fried fish dlrs
459	Dye	Grocer
469	Iron, Steel & Metal Dressers & kindered	
	Society	
489	Wright J. & Sons Ltd.	
		Haulage Contractors

Bee Street

	Carbrook Hall Filling Station	
	Petrol Service Station	
537	Carbrook Hall Hotel	Public House
	Marcroft R. S. Ltd.	Slaters
553	Dr Nicholls/Oates	Physcn. & Surgn.
555	Hague	Midwife

Goulder Terrace

Warden Street

603	Clark	Grocer
611	Rhodes	Shopkeepers
617	Royal Hotel	Public House

Mons Street

631	Stuart	Fried Fish Dlr.

637	Priestley	Shopkeeper

Southern Street

639/641	Dunn	Dressmaker
649	Max	Turf commission agent
651	Union Inn	Public House
661	Salt	Confectioner
663	Buttery	Turf Commision agt.
665	Banks G. Ltd.	Builders
669	Wheatley	Shopkeeper
671	Banks G. Ltd.	Builders
673	Knowles	Tobacconists
675	Hall	Hairdressers
677	Edythe,	Ladies' Hairdresses
677a	Wilson Brothers	Sheet Metal Workers
679	Fielos	Fried Fish Dlr.

Attercliffe Common

even numbers

Kirkbridge Road

12-14	Ferner P. & Sons Ltd.	
	Wholesale Tobacconists	
16-18	Murat	Cycle Agent & Dealer
20	Samon B	Cafe
22	Sound Upholstery	
24	Cunningham	Toy Dealer

Fell Road

28-30	Clark	Grocer
32	Slack	Baker
34	Townend	Furniture Dealer
36	Caryll	Draper
38	Rimmington	Hairdresser
40	Huddart	Hardware Dealer
42	Michaels,	bargain furnaturishers

Howden Road

48	Rossingtons	Fancy Goods
50	Caplan	Watch Repairer
52	Rossingtons	Fancy Goods
54	Burnham	Grocer
56	Avrils	Fancy repository
58	Drury	Earthen ware Dealers
60	Kay	Fruitr.
62	Thorpe	Hairdresser
64	Hartle	Draper
66	Bool	General Dealer

Whitworth Lane

68	Summerhayes	Fried Fish Dealer
70	Intaz	Grocer
72-74	Car spares	
76-78	Old Gate Inn	Public House
82	Burnham	Grocer
82a	Caravan Supplies	
	Timber Merchants	
86-88	Wainwright	Physician & Surgeon.
86-88	Gething	Physician & Surgeon.
90	Fane	Hardware Dlr.
92	Phoenix Cleaners	Dyers & Cleaners
94	Collette	Florist
98	Robins	Ladies Hairdresses

100	Malik M.S	
102	Thorpe	Butcher
104	Gelsthorpe	Confectioner
106	Ibbottson	Turf Commission Agt
108	Platt	Grocer
110	Garrett	Greengrocer
112	Buckley	Stationer
	Attercliffe Pavilion	
	Heeley & Amalgamated	Cinemas
122	Thorp	Dental Agt.
124	Brashaw Brothers	Newsagents
126	Salutation Inn	Public House

Coleridge Road & Amberley Road

130-132	Bow Vaa	Restaurant
134	Fateh	Hairdresser
136	Abbott	Wool Repository
138	Whiting	Watchmaker
142	Continental Traders	
146	Young	Ladies hairdressers
152	Valentine A. & L.	Drapers
156	Ashton	Fried Fish Dealer
158	Shaw	Shopkeeper
160	Hinchliffe	Boot Repairer
164	Sporne	Fruitr.
166-168	Travis	Tailors
172	Durbarry	Gowns
178	Nelson	Shopkeeper

Berkley Road

184	Patel	Grocer
186	Wilson	Fried Fish Dlr.
188	Hamid	Grocer
190	Cowley	Ladies Hairdresser
192	Rutherford	Confectioners
194	Northern Vision co.	

Belmoor Road

198	Northern Vision Co. Ltd.	
200	Senior	Dentist
206	Pearson	China Dlr.
208	Flather	Fried Fish Dealer
210	Sherwood	Greengrocer
212	Coates	Joinery Supplies
214	Fox	Ladies Hairdressers
218	Wagstaff	Woodworkers' Supplies

Terry Street

	Carbrook County Junior Schools	
282	Botros	Physician & Surgeon
286	Sayles	Confectioners
288	Berrisford	Fried Fish Dlr.

Carltonville Road

290	Mawson & Sons	Boot Repairers
292-298	Cosy Furnishing Co.	
		Furniture Dlrs.
300	Gallon's Ltd.	Grocers
302	Stones	Ladies Hairdresser
310	Shultz	Butcher
312	Simpson E. & B.	Drapers
314	Collins	Confectioners
316	Dixon Driving School	

318	Wistow	Fruitir.
320-324	Sullivan Ltd.	Cycle Dlrs.
326-328	Whyman	Grocer
330	Pashley	Leather Dlr.
332	Renshaw	General dlr
334	Smith	Motor Cycle Accessories

Goulder Place

336	Gilbert	Stationers
336	Gay cards	Stationers
338	Bramhall	Cafe
340	Burton	Butcher
342	Broughton Inn	Public House

Broughton Lane

366	Stoppard	Draper
368	Lockwood	Plumber
370	Hewitt	Baker

Clifton Street 372

372	Stenton M. & Co.	
		Ale & Stout Bottlers

Newton Terrace

St. Bartholomew Church
Pheasant Recreation Ground
Pheasant   Public House
Associated Electrical Industries
(Manchester) Ltd.
Ward Thomson W. Ltd.
                    Scrap Iron Dealers

The houses and Lambpool at the top of Janson Street